21st Century
Basic Skills
Library

# FLOODS!

by Cecilia Minden, PhD

Cherry Lake Publishing • Ann Arbor, Michigan

Published in the United States of America
by Cherry Lake Publishing
Ann Arbor, Michigan
www.cherrylakepublishing.com

Photo Credits: Cover and page 1, ©Erwin Wodicka/Shutterstock,
Inc.; page 4, ©Steve Cukrov/Shutterstock, Inc.; page 6, ©Tad Denson/
Shutterstock, Inc.; page 8, ©Four Oaks/Shutterstock, Inc.; page 10,
©50u15pec7a70r/Shutterstock, Inc.; page 12, ©Caitlin Mirra/Shutterstock,
Inc.; page 14, ©Gaydukov Sergey/Shutterstock, Inc.; page 16, ©iofoto/
Shutterstock, Inc.; page 18, ©GeoM/Shutterstock, Inc.; page 20,
©Global Warming Images/Alamy.

Library of Congress Cataloging-in-Publication Data
Minden, Cecilia.
  Floods!/by Cecilia Minden.
     p. cm.—(21st century basic skills library level 2)
  Includes bibliographical references and index.
  ISBN-13: 978-1-60279-866-3 (lib. bdg.)
  ISBN-10: 1-60279-866-4 (lib. bdg.)
  1. Floods—Juvenile literature. I. Title. II. Series.
  GB1399.M54 2010
  363.34'93—dc22                                    2009048582

Cherry Lake Publishing would like to acknowledge
the work of The Partnership for 21st Century Skills.
Please visit www.21stcenturyskills.org for more information.

Printed in the United States of America
Corporate Graphics Inc.
July 2010
CLFA07

# TABLE OF CONTENTS

5 **It's a Flood!**

7 **Why Do Floods Happen?**

17 **What Can You Do?**

22 Find Out More

22 Glossary

23 Home and School Connection

24 Index

24 About the Author

# It's a Flood!

The river is **overflowing**. It's a flood!

How does a flood happen?

What can you do?

# Why Do Floods Happen?

Floods happen when there is too much water.

Storms, **hurricanes**, and even snow can make floods.

Storms can bring a lot of rain.

The rain needs a place to go.

Too much rain floods the land.

**Levees** hold river water where it belongs.

Too much rain makes rivers overflow.

Hurricanes bring **ocean** water onto the land.

The water floods homes and roads.

Snow in the **mountains** melts in the spring.

This fills up rivers and **streams**.

# What Can You Do?

Help your family plan for a flood.

Make a list of things to do.

Listen to weather reports.

*Flood Watch* means there may be a flood.

*Flood Warning* means you may need to leave your home.

*Flash Flood Warning* means get out! Get to higher ground right away.

Stay safe!

# Find Out More

## BOOK

Doeden, Matt. *Floods*. Mankato, MN: Capstone Press, 2009.

## WEB SITE

**Federal Emergency Disaster Agency (FEMA) for Kids**
*www.fema.gov/kids/floods.htm*
Discover interesting facts and games that help you learn more about floods.

# Glossary

**hurricanes** (HUR-uh-kanez) severe storms with winds higher than 74 miles per hour

**levees** (LEV-eez) banks built up along rivers to prevent flooding

**mountains** (MOUN-tuhnz) high pieces of land

**overflowing** (oh-ver-FLOH-ing) flowing over the edges of something

**ocean** (OH-shuhn) the saltwater that covers three fourths of Earth's surface

**streams** (STREEMZ) small flowing bodies of water

# Home and School Connection

Use this list of words from the book to help your child become a better reader. Word games and writing activities can help beginning readers reinforce literacy skills.

| | | | |
|---|---|---|---|
| a | higher | mountains | stay |
| and | hold | much | storms |
| away | home | need | streams |
| be | homes | needs | the |
| belongs | how | ocean | there |
| bring | hurricanes | of | things |
| can | in | onto | this |
| do | is | out | to |
| does | it | overflow | too |
| even | it's | overflowing | up |
| family | land | place | warning |
| fills | leave | plan | watch |
| flash | levees | rain | water |
| flood | list | reports | weather |
| floods | listen | right | what |
| for | lot | river | when |
| get | make | rivers | where |
| go | makes | roads | why |
| ground | may | safe | you |
| happen | means | snow | your |
| help | melts | spring | |

# Index

Flash Flood
 Warnings, 21
Flood Warnings, 19
Flood Watches, 19

homes, 13, 19
hurricanes, 7, 13

levees, 11

mountains, 15

oceans, 13
overflow, 5, 11

planning, 17

rain, 9, 11
rivers, 5, 11, 15

roads, 13

snow, 7, 15
storms, 7, 9
streams, 15

water, 7, 9, 11,
 13, 15
weather reports, 19

# About the Author

Cecilia Minden is the former Director of the Language and Literacy Program at the Harvard Graduate School of Education. She currently works as a literacy consultant for school and library publishers and is the author of more than 100 books for children.